THE SECRET WORLD OF ANIMALS

This book takes you inside the secret hideaways of many kinds of animals. You'll discover a hidden world where animals rest, take cover from harsh weather, escape enemies, and raise their young. Unusual illustrations give you inside views of many animal homes.

Down and out into the night, a deer mouse scurries from a tree hole. During the day, it rests there, in a nest lined with dry grass, moss, and feathers.

COVER: A red fox pup peeks from the den where it was born. It is just beginning to explore the outside world.

BOOKS FOR WORLD EXPLORERS
NATIONAL GEOGRAPHIC SOCIETY

CONTENTS

"How can you sleep?" young burrowing owls seem to ask. Perhaps the adult is exhausted by the chore of feeding them. If danger threatens, the owlets will dash back into their burrow.

Copyright © 1986 National Geographic Society
Library of Congress CIP data: page 104

JERRY L. FERRARA

ENTERING THE
SECRET WORLD
AN INTRODUCTION

The secret world of animals is the world of their shelters, hiding places, and nurseries. Forests, meadows, deserts, and mountains—as well as your own backyard—contain the trees, burrows, and caves that many kinds of animals call home. The home life of these creatures is full of surprises for most humans, who are seldom aware of the hidden world of animals. Even if you have seen a hole in the ground or in a tree trunk, you've probably not seen what life is like inside it.

Thanks to the work of scientists and photographers, you now can see what goes on in a woodpecker hole, an underground yellow jacket nest, and a badger sett—to name just a few of the animal homes in this book. Illustrations reveal animals resting, escaping enemies or extreme weather, and raising their young. Some use their shelters year-round. Others use them only during certain

▽ *Watching a gopher tortoise near its burrow entrance, 13-year-old Lara Partin, of Melrose, Florida, wonders about its underground life.*

▽ *Anybody home? A hole in a snow-covered bank is a sign that a bear may be using the bank as a den. It is a dry, snug place for a winter sleep.*

RICHARD P. SMITH/TOM STACK & ASSOCIATES

▷ *Shown greatly enlarged and with a load of sand in its jaws, a red harvester ant emerges from the nest it is digging.*

FIONA SUNQUIST

ROBERT AND LINDA MITCHELL (RIGHT)

4

seasons of the year. Still others need shelters only when they are raising young. Some animals have adapted, over time, to living almost their entire lives underground. Others make shelters that are used as "hotels" by members of different species.

To enable you to peer directly into an underground burrow or to peek inside a nest chiseled in a tree trunk, photographers sometimes removed parts of the earth or the tree. Then they placed see-through material there. The resulting photographs show activities inside burrows or nests that are seldom seen by humans. When it was necessary to disturb an animal home, the photographers were careful not to harm the animals living there. Sometimes, paintings are used to show how an animal's shelter is constructed and what goes on inside.

This book provides you with close-up views of the private lives of many animals. Now when you look at a hole in the ground or in a hollow tree, you'll have a better idea of what goes on inside. With this new knowledge and your own imagination, your world will expand to include many of the hidden places where animals live.

▷ *A small songbird cares for its eight hungry young in a cavity in a dead tree. To make this picture, the photographer cut away part of the tree trunk. Then he built a wooden tunnel and placed it between his camera and the nest. Through the tunnel, he took pictures like this one.*

▽ *A cutaway shows what part of a European rabbit's tunnel system looks like. Careful research has made it possible for you to view such slices of life from the secret world of animals.*

HIDEAWAYS

YEAR-ROUND

By Sharon L. Barry

Many kinds of animals use hideaways year-round. Their shelters help protect them from enemies and from harsh weather. The shelters also provide safe, cozy places for the animals to sleep and to raise their young. Yet, these animals also spend much of their time

outside. They must leave their secret world to find food.

These two young banner-tailed kangaroo rats live with their mother in a maze of tunnels inside a mound. If you were to visit a desert in the southwestern United States or northern Mexico, you might see such mounds. They can be up to 2 feet ($\frac{1}{2}$ m)* high and 15 feet ($4\frac{1}{2}$ m) wide. Each is usually occupied by a single bannertail unless babies are present.

Like many desert animals, banner-tailed kangaroo rats stay underground during the day. At night, they go outside to look for food. As evening temperatures drop, moisture from the air forms on plants and seeds. They absorb some of this moisture, and bannertails take in the life-giving water as they eat. These small rodents store large quantities of seeds

Two young banner-tailed kangaroo rats greet each other at an entrance to the mound where they were born. Their desert home (above) may have as many as 12 openings. Although bannertails prefer to live alone, young ones stay with their mother until they are able to care for themselves.

*METRIC FIGURES IN THIS BOOK HAVE BEEN ROUNDED OFF.

▽ *Sniffing and snorting, a six-banded armadillo searches for food. Most armadillos feed under cover of darkness. Ants, termites, and worms are their favorite foods.*

inside their mounds. There, the seeds absorb even more moisture from the soil. The plants and seeds provide bannertails with the water they need. These desert animals never have to take an actual drink of water.

Like bannertails, most armadillos (ar-muh-DILL-ohz) live alone, except for females with young. Armadillos live in grassy areas and in open forests from the southern United States through most of South America. Each animal digs several simple burrows within its territory and uses them for sleeping during the day. At night, the armadillo goes outside to feed. If threatened by enemies, such as dogs and bobcats, it heads for its nearest burrow. If one isn't close enough, this animal can dig one fast. It can completely bury itself within two minutes.

Not all burrow users make their own shelters. For example, on African grasslands, warthogs often take over burrows that have been abandoned by termite-eating animals called aardvarks (ARD-varks). Although warthogs graze in groups during the day, they occupy separate shelters at night, except for females with young.

▷ *Tsk, tsk. Two pairs of curved tusks and a wide snout are all you can see of a warthog in an abandoned aardvark burrow. When threatened, warthogs often back into burrows so that their fierce-looking tusks point out.*

▽ *Large bumps on its face give the warthog its name. A warthog uses its tusks and its shovel-like head for digging.*

△ *With skin still soft and pink, young nine-banded, or long-nosed, armadillos snuggle up to their mother. She has lined the burrow with straw and corn* husks for warmth. Underground, the young are safe from bobcats and other enemies. Long-nosed armadillos are the only kind found in the wild in the United States.

10

Female warthogs use the burrows as nurseries. Underground, the young are safe from the extreme changes in temperature that occur on the African grasslands. The burrows also provide shelter from predators. When chased by lions or other large cats, warthogs flee to the nearest vacant shelter. A mother protects her young by allowing them to scramble in first. She then backs in and points her sharp tusks outward, toward the enemy.

You wouldn't want to approach a warthog's burrow, but you've probably walked right on top of other animal homes without even noticing. Several kinds of crabs dig burrows along the seashore. The adult ghost crab, for example, digs its hideaway in sand above the high-tide line. It will drown if it is underwater too long. During the heat of the day, the ghost crab stays underground. For extra protection from heat and enemies, it plugs its burrow opening with damp sand. Some crabs, like the square crab of Europe, prefer to burrow into sand or mud underwater.

Another secret world of year-round hideaways is high above the ground, inside trees. Each night, while you're sleeping, many kinds

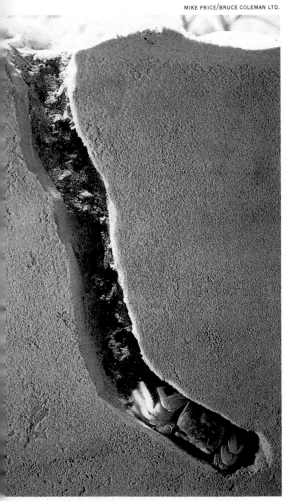

MIKE PRICE/BRUCE COLEMAN LTD.

◁ *If you could view a slice of beach anywhere from the state of Delaware to Brazil, a country in South America, you would probably see ghost crabs in their burrows. These may be 4 feet (1 m) deep. Ghost crabs spend much of their time repairing their homes or digging new ones.*

▷ *With eyes on stalks, a square crab surveys the beach at low tide. Usually, its burrow is underwater. Like the ghost crab, the square crab digs a tunnel just the width of its body and lives there alone.*

of mammals—animals that nurse their young—pop out of holes in hollow trees. They spend the night searching for food. Then, as daylight dawns, these nocturnal—or nighttime—creatures return to their hidden tree houses to sleep. Some of the tree houses are holes formed where limbs have broken away or where rot has attacked a tree. Others are holes carved out by woodpeckers.

Mammals search for vacant holes of the right size and settle in. Tree houses, like underground homes, protect animals from bad weather and from most enemies. They're also safe places to raise young. Usually bits of bark and rotten wood pad the floors of tree dens, making them comfortable places to sleep. Some mammals bring in extra bedding. Opossum mothers line their dens with leaves. They carry the leaves by gripping them with their tails against their stomachs. Flying squirrels use bark, moss, feathers, and fur to make cozy nests in abandoned woodpecker holes.

Since these tree-dwelling mammals are active at night, chances are you've never seen them in the wild—with the possible exception of the raccoon. Raccoons live in cities and towns as well as

△ *A tree hole frames a fisher's face. Related to weasels, fishers use tree dens for sleeping during the day and for raising their young.*

◁ *After dark, a bush baby prepares to leave its shelter. Large eyes and ears help it locate insects as it leaps from limb to limb. Bush babies live in Africa. They are related to monkeys.*

14

◁ *Where's mom? A curious ten-week-old Virginia opossum is now too large to ride on its mother's back while she hunts. She has left her young in a leaf-lined tree cavity.*

▷ *About to glide off in search of nuts and insects, a flying squirrel gets ready to leap from its tree house—an abandoned woodpecker hole.*

▽ This raccoon cub is safe in a tree den. Soon, it will begin to explore the world outside. Its mother will stay nearby to protect it from predators. Raccoons sometimes make nests in the basements, attics, or chimneys of houses.

ART WOLFE

▷ High above the ground, raccoon cubs enjoy the view with their mother after nursing. Female raccoons give birth in the spring. The cubs live with their mother for about a year.

in forests and marshes throughout much of North and South America. Although usually active at night, they sometimes hunt for food during the day. Raccoons take shelter in a variety of places, such as caves and even basements and attics. But their favorite hideaways are high in hollow trees.

Now, take a look at another mammal that usually hunts at night—the badger. The badger, however, is not a tree dweller. It makes its home underground and is, perhaps, the champion of diggers. Badgers dig to get their food as well as to make their homes. They have long, curved claws that are well suited to the job. Badgers can dig faster in loose soil than a human can shovel. Their short legs allow them to travel easily through underground passages.

Although similar in appearance, the North American badger and the European badger have very different life-styles. North American badgers live on dry plains and on open prairies. Except for mothers with cubs, these badgers live alone. In the summer, a North American badger may dig a new burrow every day for resting and for getting out of the sun. In winter, this kind of badger spends

BILL IVY

16

Uh-oh! What's this masked bandit up to? Waking up, that's what. Where winters are harsh, raccoons often sleep through the coldest times. Upon waking, they're hungry. Nimble paws help raccoons catch frogs and other prey.

most of its time in a single burrow, sleeping and resting.

European badgers, on the other hand, prefer hilly areas with loose soil—often at the edge of the woods. These badgers live in family groups in burrow systems called setts. Two to three adult males and several adult females with their young may occupy a sett. The sett may have three or four levels and be 15 feet (4¹/₂ m) deep. An average sett has five to eight openings, more than 100 feet (30 m) of tunnels, and 10 to 20 rooms. Generation after generation of these badgers may use the same sett for hundreds of years.

European rabbits, like badgers, prefer loose soil for digging their underground homes. These rabbits live in large, rambling burrow systems called warrens. Warrens may be as deep as 10 feet (3 m). Inside them, winding tunnels connect several sleeping rooms. Unlike mother badgers, mother rabbits usually dig nesting burrows that are separate from the warren. In these nurseries, the babies are safe from male members of the warren that might harm them. North American rabbits don't dig warrens. Instead, they scratch out shallow cavities, called forms, in the ground. *(Continued on page 22)*

△ *In a field of poppies, a North American badger shows off its digging skills. Badgers can tunnel out of sight in just two minutes. Their short legs help them move through low underground passages.*

◁ *Dig this! A honey badger goes after a burrowing lizard. Honey badgers live in Africa and Asia. As you might guess, these badgers like honey.*

ANTHONY BANNISTER

◁ *A young North American badger emerges from its burrow. Sharp claws make good digging tools. Along with the claws, its teeth can be used as weapons in self-defense.*

▷ *Stripes of a different pattern mark the slightly larger European badger. On the next two pages, find out how it spends its nights and what its underground home looks like.*

19

BURROWING BADGERS

European badgers build large underground burrow systems called setts. Several families may occupy one sett. During the day, the badgers stay inside, sleeping or resting. At dusk, they come out to eat, to exercise, and to gather clean bedding.

This painting shows a badger sett in England in

early spring. Part of the earth on the hillside has been removed so that you can look into the secret, underground world of the badger.

Inside, tunnels connect a series of chambers, or rooms. The badgers use some of them as bedrooms. They use others as nurseries. These rooms contain grass and other plant material. Rooms without bedding are no longer in use. Several young, called

20

cubs, play in a nursery chamber located under a large tree. The tree roots help support the ceiling of the nursery. Badgers build nursery chambers in the upper level of a sett so that rainwater can drain off.

The badgers come and go through several openings. Near the openings are mounds of dirt and old bedding material, called spoils. At right, dirt flies as a badger opens an old entrance. At left,

a female backs into her nursery chamber. She has fresh bedding material tucked under her chin.

Near a tree, two badgers groom themselves before they set out in search of food. One badger stretches its muscles against a tree trunk. Another heads toward a well-worn path to the pastures beyond. There, it will find a plentiful supply of earthworms—the European badger's favorite food.

(Continued from page 18) Grass or other plants usually hide the forms of North American rabbits.

Animals that live together in family groups, such as European badgers and European rabbits, are called social animals. Another kind of social animal is the black-tailed prairie dog. Prairie dogs live in huge underground communities called towns. Each town is divided into neighborhoods. Several family groups, called coteries (COAT-uh-reez), make up a neighborhood. A coterie usually has one adult male and several adult females with their young. Each coterie has its own burrow system, which it defends against other coteries. The burrow system has tunnels leading to chambers used for sleeping, for storing food, and for raising young. There are usually toilet areas, ledges for turning around, and even listening posts. At listening posts, prairie dogs keep an ear out for enemies above ground. In Chapter 5, you'll read more about prairie dogs and some of the animals that share living space with them.

One animal that often moves into prairie dog towns is the burrowing owl. It may also take over burrows (Continued on page 26)

▽ *A European rabbit enjoys a grassy snack. Rabbits come out during the evening and early morning to nibble on plants.*

IAN BEAMES/ARDEA LONDON LTD.

G. I. BERNARD/OXFORD SCIENTIFIC FILMS

△ *Two-week-old European rabbits huddle in a nesting den dug by their mother. She has lined the nest with grass, moss, and fur. Before dawn, she nurses her kittens. When the mother leaves the den, she hides the entrance.*

▷ *Ears perked, a European rabbit listens for danger at the opening to its shelter. European rabbits live in a maze of underground burrows, called warrens. There, the rabbits hide from enemies such as dogs, foxes, weasels, and hawks.*

Black-tailed prairie dog pups huddle atop a mound at an entrance to their town. The mound helps funnel fresh air into the burrow system, and it helps keep rainwater out. The prairie dogs keep the mound free of vegetation so that they have a clear view. If a prairie dog spots an enemy, it barks a warning. Then all the prairie dogs dive to safety. This bark gives prairie dogs their name, but actually they're not dogs. They're large ground squirrels.

24

(Continued from page 22) abandoned by armadillos, badgers, foxes, and skunks. If no ready-made home is available, burrowing owls dig their own, using their long, sharp talons, or claws.

Burrowing owls are small, long-legged birds. Mated pairs stay together for life. Inside their burrow, they build a nest of grass, cattle droppings, and odds and ends, such as bits of bone, feathers, and corncobs. If an intruder enters the burrow, the owls defend themselves by imitating the sound of a rattlesnake.

Burrowing owls usually hunt at dusk for insects, mice, and other small animals. When there are young to feed, the adults hunt around the clock. At times, the owls store food in the burrow for later use. In areas where food is plentiful, several families may live in neighboring burrows. Such groups are called colonies. During cold weather, groups of owls sometimes live together for warmth.

Some of the most complex hidden shelters are built by rather small animals—ants and wasps. There are more than 6,000 kinds of ants. Many—including those in your backyard—excavate huge underground shelters with many tunnels (Continued on page 30)

JERRY L. FERRARA

△ *Cricket, anyone?*
Cooing softly at the entrance to its underground home, an adult burrowing owl announces its arrival to hungry young inside. Burrowing owl parents take turns caring for their offspring.

▷ *Six burrowing owl chicks escape their crowded home, but they stay near the entrance for safety. When their parents return with food, the chicks may knock each other over in their eagerness to eat.*

26

◁ *Two Japanese harvester ants—shown several times life-size—haul a seed to their nest. Harvester ants use some seeds immediately. They store others in a network of underground rooms.*

▽ *This 12-foot (4-m) slice of earth reveals the home of Japanese harvester ants. Off the main tunnel is a network of chambers for resting, for storing food, and for raising young.*

◁ *Harvester ants stack seeds in a storage chamber. Workers—all female—will crush the seeds with their powerful jaws and chew them into a paste called ant bread. Other workers feed this bread to developing ants, called larvae (LAAR-vee). It is also food for the adults of the colony.*

(Continued from page 26) and chambers. Ants construct these nests by carrying away tiny bits of dirt in their jaws.

Different members of an ant colony have different jobs. One important job is gathering food from outside. Harvester ants, for example, harvest various kinds of seeds. They store some seeds but use others right away. They use all the seeds to make ant bread—a food made by chewing the seeds and mixing them with saliva.

Another kind of underground ant is the honey ant. These ants collect nectar from plants. They also gather honeydew, a sweet liquid deposited on plants by tiny insects called aphids (A-fidz). Honey ants use certain members of their own colony, called repletes (rih-PLEETS), as storage tanks for the sweet liquid. Workers keep feeding the repletes until their abdomens swell up like tiny balloons. When sources of nectar and honeydew are scarce, members of the colony stroke the repletes. This stroking signals the repletes to regurgitate, or bring up, "honey" for the hungry ants to drink.

Some kinds of ants don't live underground. Janitor ants, for example, make their homes in hollow twigs and branches. To guard

JANITOR ANTS CALL TWIGS HOME

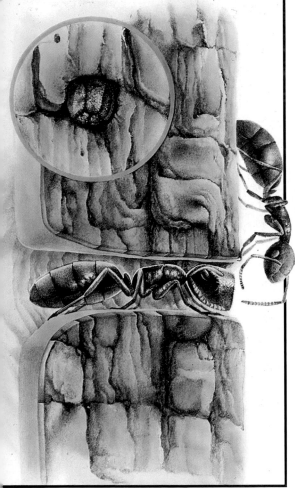

Janitor ants build nests inside the twigs of certain kinds of trees. Tiny holes lead inside. To prevent enemies and strangers from entering, soldier members of a janitor ant colony take turns plugging the holes with their heads. The safety of the colony depends on the soldier ants. The painting at left shows a soldier ant, much larger than life-size, performing her job. A worker ant seeks admission. She uses her antennae (an-TEN-ee) to tap a signal—a kind of secret password—on the soldier's head. The soldier ant recognizes both the password and the smell of the worker. She will back up just enough to let the worker enter and then quickly plug the hole again. Her large, flat head blends with the bark. The smaller drawing shows how her head looks from outside.

△ *Their abdomens swollen, honey ants hang from the domed ceiling of a chamber in their underground nest. Called repletes, these ants have the job of storing in their bodies sweet juices collected by other workers. When nectar and honeydew are scarce, the colony will use the stored juices as emergency food. When given a signal, a replete regurgitates, or brings up, "honey" for other members of the colony to drink.*

ART BY ROBERT HYNES, ADAPTED FROM J. SZABÓ-PATAY

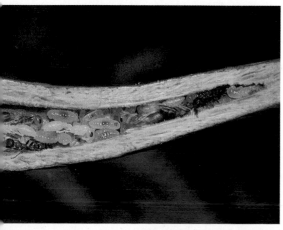

◁ *A thorn of an acacia (uh-KAY-shuh) tree makes a snug home for adult acacia ants and their young. One side of the thorn has been removed to show ants in various stages of development.*

▷ *Hungry for honey, an ant prepares to leave its nest in an acacia thorn. The ant helps protect the tree, its source of honey, by attacking leaf-eating insects.*

ROBERT AND LINDA MITCHELL (ABOVE AND RIGHT)

the entrances to their twig homes, soldier janitor ants serve as door-keepers. They have large, flat heads for plugging the holes that lead into their nests.

Like ants, some kinds of wasps are social animals. A social wasp called a yellow jacket sometimes builds its home underground in a burrow left by another animal. The queen builds a nest of paper, which she makes by chewing wood and other plant material and mixing them with saliva. She hangs the nest from roots at the top of the burrow. Then she lays eggs in the cells, or small compartments, of the nest. These eggs produce worker wasps that enlarge the nest and the burrow as the queen lays more eggs. Eventually, the nest may contain more than 2,000 wasps and be the size of a football.

In this chapter, you have looked into many year-round hide-aways. Some of them are in twigs or high in hollow tree trunks. Others are deep underground. All serve as resting places, as shelters from enemies and bad weather, and even as nurseries. They are secret worlds for the animal inhabitants. Just about the only reason these animals leave home is to find food!

WASPS THAT LIVE UNDERGROUND

After hunting for food, wasps called yellow jackets return to their nest in a burrow (right). A mouse or other small mammal had abandoned its underground home. In early spring, the queen wasp took over the burrow and *started a nest there. She attached it to plant roots in the ceiling of the burrow. Gradually, her worker offspring enlarged the nest to the size of a football (above). A section of it has been cut away to show the layers of cells inside.*

32

SURVIVING THE
SEASONS

By Jan Leslie Cook

Carrying a nut in its mouth, a chipmunk heads for home. In late summer and early fall, chipmunks get ready for the cold months ahead. They store extra food in their burrows, and they eat until they are fat. They also spend much time preparing their under-

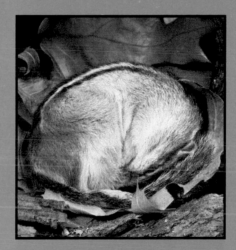

ground shelters. A chipmunk's burrow system has a main tunnel up to 15 feet (5 m) long. This tunnel usually goes to a nesting chamber lined with dry leaves and grass. From there, shorter tunnels lead to chambers used for storing food. In its snug burrow, a chipmunk sleeps through much of the winter.

Just as extremely cold weather is a threat to animals in some climates, extremely hot weather threatens animals in other climates. They, too, survive by sleeping. In this chapter, you will peek into some of the secret shelters that help animals live through extremes of cold or heat.

Many animals survive extremely cold weather by going into hibernation—periods of inactivity that occur frequently throughout the winter. Several times during the cold months, hibernating

Preparing for winter, a chipmunk carries a nut to its burrow (left). The chipmunk makes many trips to its underground home each day to store food. When winter arrives and food is scarce, the chipmunk curls up (above) and goes to sleep. It awakens occasionally for a snack.

BRECK P. KENT (BOTH)

▽ Sniffing the spring air, a chipmunk peeks from its burrow after a long winter. Soon the chipmunk will begin its warm-weather work of storing food and tidying its burrow.

animals may arouse and become active. Then they go back into hibernation. During hibernation, an animal's heartbeat slows down, as does its rate of breathing. Its body temperature also drops. Different kinds of animals experience different degrees of hibernation. The body temperature of raccoons, for example, drops very little. They may become sluggish, but they sleep only during extremely cold times. The temperatures of some other mammals, such as marmots and ground squirrels, drop very low, and these animals remain in hibernation for long periods. Other animals—reptiles and amphibians, for example—remain completely inactive all winter or until the weather warms up.

Because all of their bodily functions slow down, hibernating animals require very little energy to stay alive. Their low body temperatures and their reduced need for energy help them survive periods of cold and lack of food.

Marmots, like chipmunks, hibernate in underground burrows. Where winters are harsh, they stay underground for as long as seven months. Twenty or more of these *(Continued on page 40)*

△ Underground for nearly seven months, a marmot rests in its grass-lined burrow. Marmot burrows have many entrances. During early spring outings, marmots seem to be able to remember the locations of the entrances—even those under several feet of snow.

▷ A furry marmot with a mouthful of grass prepares to line its burrow. The grass will help protect it against winter cold. Once inside for the winter, marmots may stuff the entrance tunnels with soil and rocks to shut out enemies and to block the colder outside air from entering the burrow.

36

JERRY L. FERRARA

Young marmots soak up the sun after a winter underground. For safety, they stay near the burrow. If their mother senses danger, she will give a warning whistle. Then the entire colony of marmots will dash underground.

39

(*Continued from page 36*) furry animals may live together. In the late summer and early fall, members of the marmot colony get ready for the long winter.

They play in the sun; they eat; and they prepare large, comfortable burrows with many entrances. The network of tunnels in a marmot colony may cover an area larger than a football field. Within this area, their grass-lined burrows lie several feet under the ground. Each sleeping chamber is large enough for more than one marmot. They often huddle together for warmth.

Ground squirrels, like marmots, spend the winter hibernating for days at a time. If you could pick up one of these little animals near the end of winter while it was still sleeping, you might think it was dead. It breathes only about three times a minute, and its body is cold, thin, and lightweight. Like other hibernating animals, the ground squirrel uses the fat stored in its body for nourishment.

Some kinds of bears hibernate, but their temperature drops only slightly. They make their dens in caves, in hollow logs, or beneath fallen trees. Except for females and their (*Continued on page 44*)

WARREN GARST/TOM STACK & ASSOCIATES

◁ *Curled up in a ball, a ground squirrel sleeps in its circular nest. Before cold weather set in, the squirrel dug its underground home and stored a winter food supply. A tunnel several feet long leads to the sleeping chamber, which the squirrel has lined with dry grass and leaves. This cozy lining cushions the animal's body from the cold earth all around it.*

40

MICHAEL S. QUINTON (ABOVE AND BELOW)

△ *Seeking the warmth of the sun, a ground squirrel pops up from its burrow after a winter underground. Ground squirrels always awaken slowly from their periods of hibernation. They take up to three hours to become fully alert. Now this hungry animal will search for green plants to eat.*

◁ *A snow-covered world greets a ground squirrel in winter. Like many kinds of hibernators, ground squirrels awaken several times from hibernation. They may even leave their burrows. Before going back to sleep, they usually eat a few stored nuts or seeds and tidy their nests.*

41

A LONG WINTER'S SLEEP

If you walked in the woods on a cold winter day, you might approach, without noticing, some of the animals shown here. These animals are tucked away in the cozy world of their secret shelters. In this painting, portions of the shelters have been cut away so that you can peek in. The bears and the ground

squirrel are mammals that spend all or part of the winter in hibernation. The snakes, the turtle, and the bullfrog are cold-blooded animals. They cannot produce enough heat to keep themselves warm. As long as cold weather lasts, they are completely inactive. Shelters protect all of these animals from the cold. Sometimes shelters offer protection from enemies as well.

The mother bear and her cubs stay snug in a cave. Before going into hibernation, the mother bear lined the cave floor with twigs and grass to make a dry, warm bed. Beneath the tree, in an underground burrow, a ground squirrel sleeps on a bed of grass. It has plugged the tunnel entrance with dirt to keep out enemies and the cold outside air.

Near the bears' den, masses of garter snakes are hibernating deep in rocky pits. A turtle hibernates in the bank of a pond. At the bottom of the pond, a bullfrog has buried itself under mud and dead leaves for the winter. These cold-blooded animals have taken shelter below the frost line—the point below which the ground does not freeze. To keep from freezing, they must remain there, completely inactive, until winter ends.

43

(Continued from page 40) cubs, bears hibernate alone. Every other winter, a female bear gives birth in her den to two or three furry cubs. The cubs don't hibernate that first winter. They snuggle next to their mother and nurse.

When spring arrives, the mother and her cubs leave the den in search of food. All summer, they stuff themselves with roots, grass, berries, and nuts. Their bodies become plump, and their fur grows thick. As autumn days shorten, the mother bear and her cubs eat less. They concentrate, instead, on preparing a den. This second winter is the last these cubs will spend with their mother. Next year, they will be on their own.

Where winters are cold, some kinds of bats, like some bears, hibernate in caves. There, they cling to the ceiling with their sharp claws. When they enter hibernation, their heartbeat slows down, they breathe infrequently, and their body temperature drops. Bats may hibernate for as long as a month at a time.

Unlike the bodies of bats, which are warm-blooded, the bodies of reptiles and amphibians produce very little heat. Cold-blooded

▽ *Taking a break from hibernation, a black bear digs in a snowbank. Before the first snow, bears select their dens, often returning to the same ones used the previous winter. They may choose well-hidden caves or spaces under fallen trees. During the winter, bears awaken often. On warm days, they may leave their dens and wander about.*

WAYNE LANKINEN/VALAN

ALAN CAREY

△ *Puppy-size bear cubs huddle inside their mother's den. They were born in midwinter while their mother was hibernating. Her body supplies warmth and milk. In another two months, the cubs will leave the den with her.*

▷ *In early spring, after a long winter, a European brown bear leaves the den with her cubs. No one knows for certain what causes hibernators to awaken. It is still a mystery. Scientists think that warmer temperatures and longer days tell the animals that spring has arrived.*

creatures survive cold weather by going deep underground. To keep from freezing, they must go below the frost line—the point to which the ground freezes. There, in their hideaways, they remain dormant—completely inactive—until the weather warms up.

In parts of Manitoba, in Canada, the hibernation of large numbers of garter snakes attracts much attention each fall. Thousands of these garter snakes leave their spring and summer homes and travel as far as 10 miles (16 km) to reach the pits where they spend the winter. During their journey, these harmless reptiles crawl through yards and houses, along highways, and across fields. Their goal is to reach several deep, rock-lined pits, where they can survive Manitoba's bitterly cold winters.

The thousands of snakes that complete the journey crawl into the pits and slide under and between rocks. There, they hibernate. Months later—about three weeks after the last snow melts—the garter snakes begin to come out of the pits and return to their warm-weather homes in the marshes.

In some parts of the world, heat and dryness may be a threat to

KERRY T. GIVENS/TOM STACK & ASSOCIATES

◁ *Drops of water cover a bat hibernating in a cave. The cave provides suitable shelter because the air inside is moist and the temperature stays above freezing. The bat's heartbeat and rate of breathing have slowed down, and its body temperature has dropped.*

▷ *These bats, called little brown bats, hang upside down from the ceiling of a cave. Bats often hibernate in groups for warmth. Up to a million bats have been found in a single colony. Some bats don't hibernate. They migrate to warmer areas or live year-round in warm climates.*

46

animals—as dangerous as severe cold is in other places. Just as some animals hibernate to survive harsh cold, others estivate to survive tremendous heat. Estivation (es-tuh-VAY-shun) is a period of sleep, or inactivity, similar to hibernation. Just as with deep hibernators, the bodily functions of estivating animals slow almost to a stop. When cooler temperatures and rain return, the animals awaken and become active once again.

The African lungfish, for example, normally lives in a river or a lake and breathes with gills, as other fish do. When drought dries up its home, the lungfish buries itself in the riverbed or the lake bottom. It leaves an air vent to the surface. Then it uses an air bladder, instead of its gills, to breathe. Enclosed in a cocoon of mucus and skin, which keeps its body from drying out, this animal can estivate for several years without food or water!

The jerboa (jer-BOH-uh) is a rodent that lives in Africa. It avoids the extreme heat of summer by estivating in a burrow 5 feet (1½ m) deep. The burrow stays much cooler than the sun-baked surface of the desert. In deserts, water is usually scarce. (Continued on page 52)

▽ *A biologist measures the temperature of a 10-foot-deep (3-m) pit in Manitoba, in Canada. Every fall, thousands of garter snakes travel many miles to pits in this area. In deep cracks between rocks, they hibernate all winter. Scientists are trying to learn how the snakes find the same pits each year.*

N. G. S. PHOTOGRAPHER BIANCA LAVIES

▷ *Garter snakes crawl out of a sun-warmed pit. As many as 10,000 snakes may emerge from a single area. After coming out of hibernation, they travel up to 10 miles (16 km) to reach the marshes where they spend the spring and summer. In September, the snakes return to the same pits.*

BRECK P. KENT

△ *Young garter snakes, here with an adult, are born live— not hatched from eggs as many snakes are. Although born far from the hibernation pits, instinct will lead them there in the fall.*

A desert tortoise takes shelter from the summer sun in a shallow burrow. To protect itself from freezing winter temperatures, it digs a deeper burrow, below the frost line. A desert tortoise spends about 90 percent of its life underground.

51

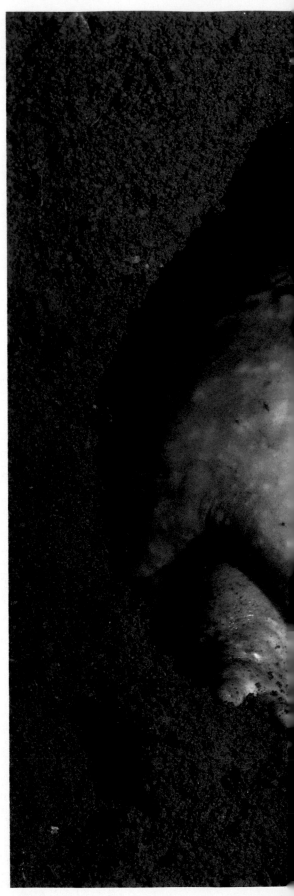

(Continued from page 48) Like many desert creatures, the jerboa gets much of the moisture it needs by eating green plants whenever they are available.

In this chapter, you've met animals that use shelters to protect themselves from extreme cold or heat, when food and water are scarce. Over time, they have adapted to their environments. Whether such animals live in mountains, forests, marshlands, or deserts, they survive unfavorable conditions by becoming inactive and using less energy.

Shelters play a large role in animal survival during these periods of inactivity. The shelters provide warmth or coolness. Sometimes they serve as places for food storage. Shelters also provide protection from enemies.

When animals enter hibernation or estivation, their bodily functions slow down—nearly to a stop. They are unable to protect themselves by running away or by fighting. Instead, they depend on shelters to hide them from their enemies. Without shelters, many of these animals could not survive.

▷ As the river dried up, this African lungfish burrowed into the riverbed, leaving itself an air vent. This kind of fish has an air bladder that acts as a lung. Encased in a cocoon of mucus, the fish can live out of water for years.

ALAN ROOT

YOFF/JACANA

△ A desert rodent called a jerboa hops toward its burrow. During extremely hot, dry spells, it goes into estivation, a period of inactivity similar to hibernation.

▷ By burying itself, this African bullfrog escapes the heat. Its body is covered with layers of mucus and old skin, which protect it from dry conditions.

52

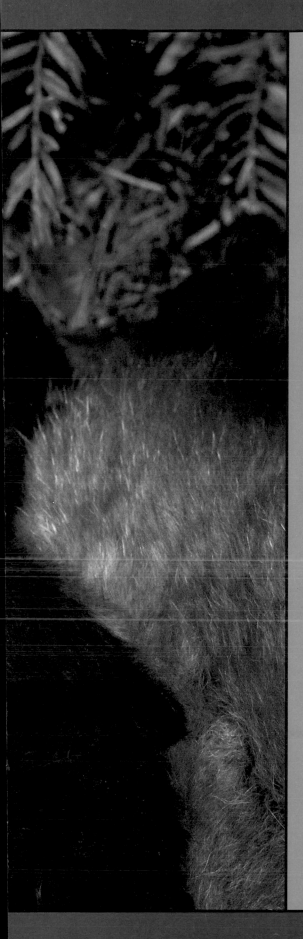

SHELTERS FOR THE

YOUNG

By Judith E. Rinard

Fuzzy little red foxes cuddle with their mother in a hidden den. In the spring, before the baby foxes were born, the mother dug the den under old logs in the woods. There, she gave birth to her young, called pups or kits. In that secret shelter, she nurses her babies

JEAN-PHILLIPPE VARIN/JACANA

and keeps them warm, wrapping her body around them like a cozy blanket. The father fox helps by bringing food for the mother.

Foxes belong to the dog family. In this chapter, you will look into shelters that members of this family provide for their helpless offspring. You will also see shelters that wild cats, birds, turtles, snails, and wasps use during the breeding season. These hideaways are places seldom seen by humans.

Shelters provide safety from enemies and from harsh weather while the young are developing. For mammals and birds, shelters may also serve as home bases for growing youngsters as they learn hunting skills and other lessons in survival.

By the time the fox pups are six weeks old, they are ready to

Two-week-old red fox pups (left) snuggle near their mother. They are still covered with dark baby fur. Older pups peek out of their den (above) and seem to say, "Let's play!" The color of their fur now matches the soil around the den opening. This camouflage helps protect them when they come out.

JANE BURTON/BRUCE COLEMAN LTD. (LEFT)

explore the outside world. By chasing each other and by pouncing on beetles and butterflies, they develop important hunting skills. Soon they will go hunting with their parents for mice, rabbits, and other small animals. The pups will gradually become expert hunters. By fall, when the family splits up, each pup will be prepared to establish its own territory and to care for itself. Although foxes may mate for life, they live alone except when raising their young.

Wolves—like foxes—are members of the dog family. But wolves live year-round in family groups called packs. A pack is made up of a male and female pair—the pack leaders—and their newborn pups, along with some of the pups' older brothers and sisters and occasionally a few aunts and uncles.

Usually, only the head female in a pack gives birth. Each spring the family group travels to an area called a homesite. Here, the female digs a den, often with the help of the pack. Later, she gives birth to five to seven young. Once the pups are about a month old and are able to eat meat, the whole pack helps care for them. Hungry pups nuzzle the mouths of wolves returning from the hunt

◁ *Digging hard, a male timber wolf takes his turn making a den where the female leader of the pack will have pups. Other members of the pack may help dig. The den will have a long tunnel leading to a birth chamber deep in the hillside. All members of the pack will help care for the young—feeding the pups, playing with them, and guarding them from bears and other enemies.*

ANIMALS ANIMALS/FRANK ROCHE

56

△ Two eight-month-old wolves (first and second from left) stand with an uncle and their parents. Born in the spring, these youngsters no longer need the protection of a den. They will learn to hunt by traveling with the pack as it tracks large prey, such as moose and elk.

◁ Recently born wolf pups huddle deep inside a den. Five to seven pups usually make up a litter. For a while, these babies will live off their mother's milk. Then, until the pups learn to hunt, pack members will feed them partially digested meat forced up from their own stomachs.

▽ "What's out there?" These coyote pups will pounce on insects—or anything that moves. Such play helps prepare them to hunt rabbits and squirrels.

to make them regurgitate (ree-GUR-juh-tate), or force up, partly digested meat. As the pack follows its food supply, or whenever danger threatens, the pups are moved to other dens in the pack's territory. When the youngsters are six months old, they no longer need the protection of a den. Then they are ready to join the adults as they hunt, learning to track and kill. Only by hunting as a pack can wolves kill large prey, such as moose and elk. It will take about two years for the pups to become expert hunters.

The coyote, the Cape hunting dog of Africa, and the Australian dingo are other kinds of wild dogs. They prepare hideaways for their young similar to those of foxes and wolves. A coyote may dig a new den or enlarge the burrow of another animal. A dingo mother may give birth in a cave or in a hollow log. In all cases, adult wild dogs do not regularly use shelters except when raising their young. Shelters provide safe places where mothers can nurse their babies undisturbed by other animals. The hideaways also protect the young while the adults are out hunting.

Wild cats, like wild dogs, give birth to their young in secret

△ Cape hunting dog pups wait at the den entrance for the pack to return with food. Like wolves, Cape hunting dogs work as a team to bring down large prey. After birth, the pups stay underground for about three weeks. When three months old, they are ready to travel with the pack.

▷ Safe and sound, newborn dingo pups nestle close to their mother. These wild dogs live in Australia. To give birth to her litter of young, this dingo chose a cave as a nursery. There, she nurses her babies and protects them from predators, such as snakes and large eagles.

shelters. There is one big difference, however. Cats are not diggers. In the spring, a mother cat finds a shelter. There, alone, she gives birth to a litter of kittens, or cubs. The shelter may be in a high cave, under a fallen tree, or in thick grass and brush.

Such shelters are needed only for a few months. When the cubs are strong enough, they leave the den and travel with their mother as she hunts. By watching her, they learn how to stalk and kill prey for themselves. Among wild cats, the mother cares for the young and teaches them to hunt. The father usually does not stay with the family. As the mother and her cubs travel around her territory, they rest in temporary shelters. When the cubs have mastered the skills they need, they go off to establish their own hunting grounds.

For the lynx and other cats that prey on small animals, learning to hunt may take only a few months. It takes more time, however, for cats to learn how to kill large prey that can defend itself. A young mountain lion, for example, stays with its mother for almost two years—until it becomes a skilled hunter, able to survive on its own.

Mammals are not the only animals that use hideaways for their

ALAN CAREY

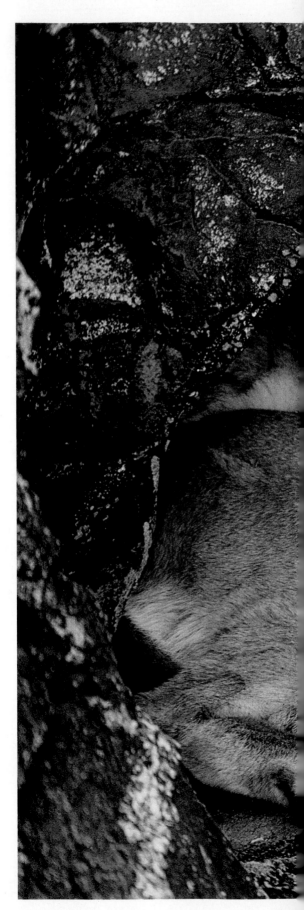

△ *Sheltered by fallen trees, a mother Canada lynx protects her cubs. She will teach them to stalk birds, rodents, and snowshoe hares. When the young are nine to ten months old, each will establish its own territory.*

▷ *Safe in a high cave, a mountain lion cub lies across its mother's body, resting during the heat of the day. Now about a year old, the cub will stay with its mother for another year, sharpening its hunting skills.*

60

young. Some birds make nest holes in cliffs, in riverbanks, or in trees. Others scrape hollows in the sand.

The Atlantic puffin is a seabird well suited for digging. At nesting time, a puffin and its mate make special use of their large bills and their sharp-clawed, paddle-like feet. With these built-in tools, they dig a long tunnel into a grassy slope by the sea. A single young—called a puffling—hatches in a chamber at the end of the tunnel. There, the puffling eats fish brought by its parents and exercises by flapping its wings. One night, when it is six weeks old, the young puffin leaves the nest and plunges into the ocean. On its own, it learns to catch fish and to fly.

The bee-eater is another tunnel-making bird. Some bee-eaters live in family groups called clans. Several clans make up a colony. At egg-laying time, nonbreeding clan members help a breeding pair make its burrow. The birds begin by ramming their partly open bills against a chosen spot on a cliff. Once a hole is started, they enlarge it by pecking and scratching. Gradually, they form a tunnel as long as 6 feet (2 m). Clan members may also *(Continued on page 66)*

IAN BEAMES/ARDEA LONDON LTD.

△ *Showing off a brightly colored bill, a seabird called an Atlantic puffin looks out from its nesting burrow. With its mate, it* dug a tunnel into the cliff, using its bill as a pick and its webbed feet as shovels. One chick will hatch inside the burrow.

△ *Rows of nest holes line a cliff in Africa. Here, birds called carmine bee-eaters breed in large colonies. These birds eat bees and wasps—after removing their stingers. To tunnel into a cliff, the parent bee-eaters chip away at dirt with their bills. Then they kick it out with their feet. Relatives often help with the work. Later, they baby-sit, caring for the eggs and then for the hatchlings.*

62

J. ROBERT/JACANA

THOMAS R. HOWELL (ABOVE AND RIGHT)

◁ *An Egyptian plover chick hatches from an egg marked by a scientist. The "pebble" next to it is an unhatched egg.*

▷ *Threatened by danger, an Egyptian plover uses its bill to toss sand over a chick. The covered chick is hard for enemies to spot. A parent will also distract an enemy or, if necessary, attack it.*

Belted kingfisher chicks perch on a stick placed by the photographer in their riverbank burrow. They often line up to take food—usually small fish—from their parents. Now 22 days old, these chicks will soon be able to fly. They will stay nearby until they can catch fish for themselves.

64

(*Continued from page 62*) take turns sitting on the eggs and feeding the hatchlings. Cooperation among members of the clan gives bee-eater chicks a better chance of surviving.

Another kind of bird that makes its nest in a tunnel is the kingfisher. The male and the female burrow into the bank of a stream or a river, using their bills and feet. In a domed chamber at the end of the tunnel, the parents take turns sitting on the eggs. After their chicks hatch, both parents feed and care for them. When the young kingfishers are about a month old, they leave the nest and learn to fish for themselves. By this time, their parents are busy preparing a new nest for a second brood of chicks.

The Egyptian plover of Africa makes a very simple hideaway for its eggs. The parents scratch a shallow nest hole on a river sandbar—a ridge of sand built up by flowing water. After laying the eggs, the birds cover them with sand to protect them from enemies. But the big problem is heat. Three hours after sunrise, the sun is scorching hot. Most birds sit on their eggs to keep them warm. Egyptian plovers, however, sit on their eggs to keep them from

◁ *A common kingfisher brings home a fish to feed its hungry young. It will enter the nest through a tunnel dug into a stream bank. Both parents feed the growing chicks. To satisfy them, the parents bring home a meal about every 15 minutes.*

▷ *Inside the burrow, a kingfisher checks on its helpless, newly hatched chicks. They huddle in a hollow in the floor of the nesting chamber. They will grow no feathers for two weeks, so the parents must take turns keeping them warm. When the babies are older, they will run to the nest entrance and beg for food.*

▽ *A screech owl swoops in for a landing, carrying a caterpillar. It will make a tasty meal for the babies in the tree hole.*

overheating. The parents frequently soak their belly feathers in the river. Then they return to the nest and wet the sand that covers their eggs. The cooling water keeps the eggs from baking in the sun. They hatch in about 30 days.

Some birds find secret shelters for their young inside trees. The screech owl, for example, looks for a vacant hole in a tree. Not an excavator itself, it must find a natural hollow or a hole made by a woodpecker. In this safe, dry shelter, the mother screech owl takes charge of sitting on her eggs.

After the eggs hatch, the father brings the owlets food—mice, bats, beetles, moths, and other insects. As the young grow and need more food, the mother also hunts. Together, the parents may make 60 trips a night. Even after the owlets learn to fly, they stay near their parents until they can catch food on their own.

A pair of pileated (PIE-lee-ate-uhd) woodpeckers, using their bills, drill and carve out their own nesting hideaway. When abandoned, woodpecker holes provide homes for many other animals.

For some animals, making a shelter or *(Continued on page 72)*

△ *Two three-week-old screech owls take a break from their cramped nest. In about a week, both of them will be able to fly.*

TREE-HOLE NURSERY

A father pileated woodpecker enters a tree hole to take his turn sitting on the eggs. He and his mate chiseled the entrance and a hole about 24 inches (61 cm) deep and 8 inches (20 cm) wide. It took them nearly a month to peck out the gourd-shaped hideaway. This painting shows an inside view of the chamber where the eggs will hatch.

68

Two-week-old pileated woodpecker chicks beg for food. The father will regurgitate insects he has swallowed for them. To gather food, the parents peck under tree bark, using their tongues to pull out grubs, wood ants, and beetles.

▽ *At nesting time, a female sea turtle returns to the beach where she hatched. An ocean dweller, she somehow finds her home beach no matter how far she must swim. Then she pulls her heavy body ashore and carefully selects a nesting site.*

FRANS LANTING

▷ *After digging a pit above the high-tide line, a sea turtle lays from 100 to 200 leathery eggs about the size of Ping-Pong balls. She will pack the hole with sand and return to the sea. The yolks of the eggs are food for the developing young.*

▷ *A newly hatched sea turtle uses its flippers to push out of the sand. The tiny creature is barely 2 inches (5 cm) long, and its shell is soft. The young turtle will be easy prey for crabs and seabirds as it scrambles across the beach. Instinct, rather than its mother, will help guide it toward the ocean, its home.*

70

C. ALAN MORGAN (LEFT AND ABOVE)

(Continued from page 68) finding one is only the beginning of a long period of caring for their young. For other animals, like the land snail (right), digging a hole and laying eggs is all there is to it. That doesn't mean it's easy, however.

The female sea turtle, for example, lays her eggs on the beach where she hatched. To do so, she may have to travel through thousands of miles of ocean. Once ashore, she drags her heavy body above the high-tide line. There, she uses her rear flippers to dig a nesting pit. After laying her eggs, she fills the pit with sand. Then she returns to the sea, never to see her young.

Some insects also perform remarkable feats at egg-laying time. The female digger wasp, for example, digs a burrow for each of her eggs and stocks each burrow with food (below).

You have now looked into different kinds of shelters that animals use for their young or for their eggs. In each case, instinct guides the denning or nesting behavior of the parents. Instinct is behavior that is inherited rather than learned. It is part of nature's way of helping animal species survive from one generation to the next.

▽ *Working hard, a female digger wasp makes her way toward a burrow she has dug in the sand. She will drag the caterpillar, which she has paralyzed, into the burrow and then lay an egg on it. When the egg hatches, the emerging grub will feast on the caterpillar.*

ANIMALS ANIMALS/PATTI MURRAY

A WASP'S SECRET NURSERY

1) *A female digger wasp removes a pebble from a burrow entrance. Earlier, she dug the burrow and temporarily blocked it off.*
2) *Grasping a caterpillar, the wasp backs down into the tunnel.*
3) *She pulls the paralyzed caterpillar in after her.*
4) *The wasp lays one egg on the caterpillar's side.*
5) *She leaves the burrow and permanently closes the tunnel with pebbles.*
6) *To hide the burrow entrance, the wasp scratches sand over it.*

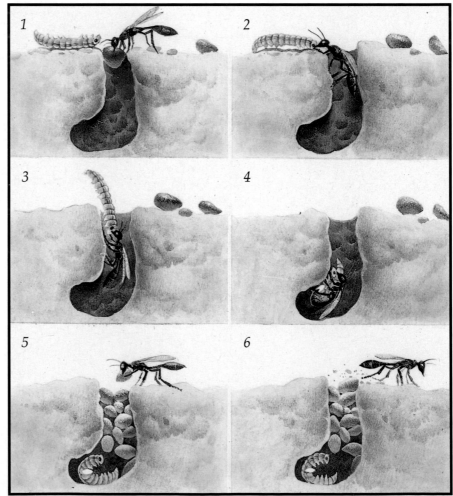

ROBERT HYNES

A land snail lays several dozen eggs. It used a muscular body part called the foot to dig the hole. In about a month, the young will hatch. Able to care for themselves, they will dig out of the nest and go their way, complete with shells.

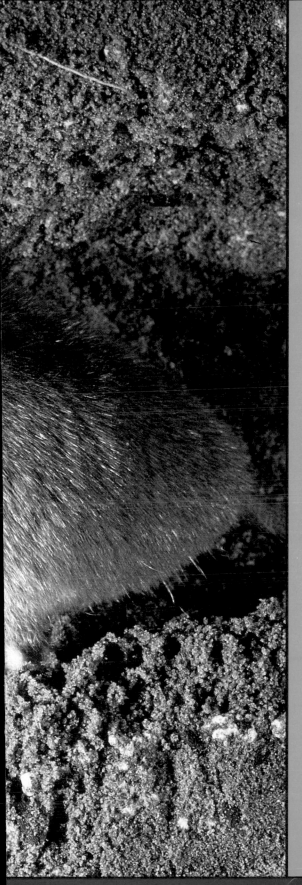

SECRETS OF LIFE

UNDERGROUND

By Robin Darcy Dennis

FIONA SUNQUIST

Dark, damp homes with dirt all around and plenty of worms and insects wouldn't appeal to human homeowners. But for some animals, such homes are perfect. In fact, many of these animals live right beneath your feet. They spend nearly all their lives underground. When it's time to eat, they tunnel for worms, insects, or roots in the soil. Tucked in snug burrows, they rest and sleep. Most even meet their mates and raise their young beneath the earth's surface.

Throughout the world, animals of various kinds live underground. In much of North America, for example, an energetic rodent called a pocket gopher burrows in meadows and forests. Small tunnel-digging moles may be right at home beneath your own backyard or garden. Under the sand of African deserts, the golden mole secretly glides. Some kinds of crickets, crayfish, and salamanders spend their lives deep within caves.

Hidden underground, these animals are usually safe from enemies that might prey on them at the surface. The surrounding earth

Raking the earth with its strong claws, a pocket gopher tunnels underground (left). As it looks for roots and bulbs to eat, it pushes soil to the surface in mound after mound (above). It hollows out living quarters deeper underground.

RAYMOND A. MENDEZ (LEFT)

also protects them from outside weather that might be too hot or too cold. These animals have developed certain physical features that help them live underground. These features, called adaptations, developed over a long period of time.

The pocket gopher, for example, is adapted to the job it does best: making tunnels. It has oversize claws for digging and large front teeth for chiseling. Its tube-shaped body easily moves backward as well as forward through narrow tunnels.

Pocket gophers occasionally make quick trips to the surface. There, they gather pieces of bark and plants. They carry this food back to their burrows in fur-lined pouches on the sides of their faces. These pouches give pocket gophers their name.

When another underground inhabitant—the mole—comes to the surface, it walks with a slow, awkward movement. That's because the mole's front legs are arranged for digging. They grow outward from its shoulders, so that it digs with a swimming motion, shoveling with one paddle-shaped paw and then the other.

Although it is small—only about the size of a chipmunk—a mole

▽ Well suited for its work, the pocket gopher is adapted to life underground. Powerful claws help it dig tunnels. If it finds roots and rocks in its path, it loosens them with long front teeth. The eyes of the pocket gopher are small and weak. They are hidden by thick, velvety fur that covers its body. This sensitive fur helps the pocket gopher feel its way along tunnels.

△ Like miniature mountains, molehills dot a field in West Germany. Tunneling European moles pushed the dirt to the surface as they dug. Although more than one mole may live in an area, each animal digs its own system of tunnels. It travels through the tunnels regularly to gather worms.

▷ In a rare moment above ground, a European mole nibbles an earthworm. A mole eats its own weight in worms, grubs, and insects every day. When worms are plentiful, a mole may store parts of live worms in its burrow for later meals.

can burrow through several feet of soft earth in a single minute. Day and night, the mole travels through its tunnels, searching for earthworms to eat. Its nose is better suited to this job than its eyes are. The mole's eyes are tiny and nearly sightless, but its sensitive nose can detect an earthworm's trail in the soil.

One kind of mole gets its name from the shape of its snout, or nose. At the end of the snout are 22 feelers. They are arranged in the shape of a star, and they can wriggle like fingers. The star-nosed mole spends part of its time hunting for food in quiet ponds or streams. With its nose, it finds tadpoles and worms along the bottom. Then it carries them back to its burrow in the side of the bank and eats them.

An unusual insect called a mole cricket tunnels like a mole and has claws similar to a mole's. The claws, as well as sharp bristles on its front legs, help it cut through soil and roots. At night, the mole cricket may fly out of its tunnels in search of food or a mate. As soon as it lands, though, it begins tunneling again.

In the Namib Desert, along the southwest *(Continued on page 82)*

△ *A digger rather than a jumper, the mole cricket lives in shallow underground burrows. It digs with its claws and with sharp bristles on its front legs.*

▷ *Sensitive feelers decorate the nose of the star-nosed mole. Their shape gives this creature its name. The star-nosed mole is the only mole that swims to find food. It spends part of its time in ponds or in streams. While swimming, it uses its nose to feel for tadpoles and worms.*

△ *The open paw of a star-nosed mole shows digging ridges on its curved "fingers."*

78

UNDERGROUND WORLD

This cutaway of a section of earth reveals a world of activity underground. A mole (far right), digging with large claws, catches an earthworm. The mole's big appetite sends it searching for food every few hours. Between hunts, it rests in its underground burrow. Another small hunter, a shrew (far left)
80

eats a beetle in a shallow burrow. Like moles, shrews need large amounts of food. They find much of their food supply—worms, insects, grubs, and plant roots and bulbs—underground.

Members of a busy ant colony move about in passages and chambers (center). Nearby, earthworms ease through the soil, looking for food. They eat decaying leaves and other plant material,

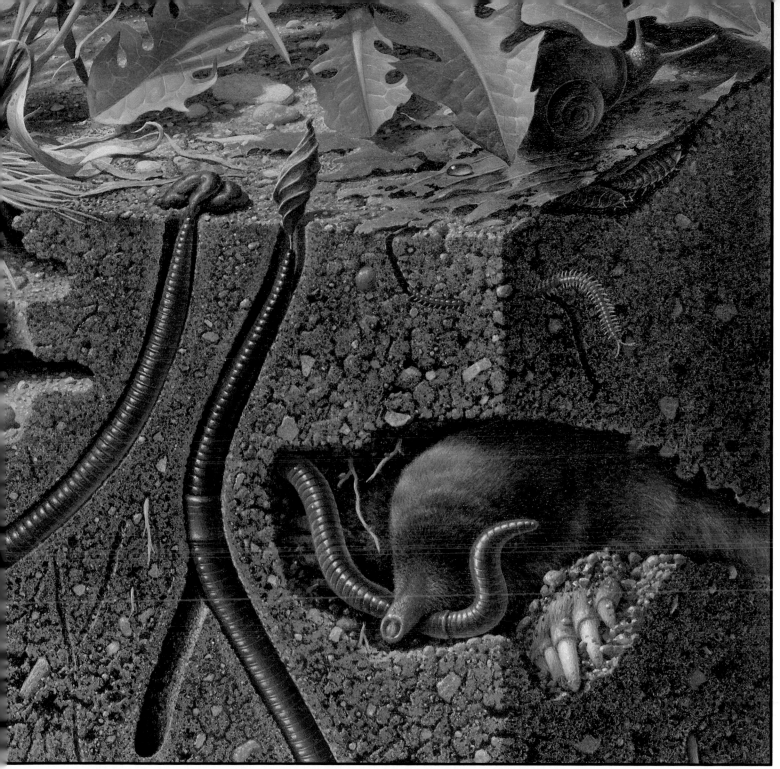

NED SEIDLER, N.G.S. STAFF

called litter. Their bodies break it down and pass the unused parts as waste, called castings. They also drag some of this litter with them as they burrow underground. As the earthworms move about, their castings mix with the soil. Rich in minerals that plants need, castings are also an important food for certain tiny animals that inhabit the soil. Centipedes and wood lice (top right) as well as creatures too

small to see with the unaided eye feed on the castings of the earthworms.

Although underground animals sometimes annoy farmers and gardeners, these creatures are very beneficial. The tunnels they dig let air and water into the ground. Their food and waste mix with the soil and enrich it. As a result, the soil nourishes plants, which supply oxygen and food for earth's animal life.

81

(Continued from page 78) coast of Africa, daytime temperatures may reach 150°F (66°C). Some animals living there avoid the heat by burrowing under the sand's surface, where it is cooler.

The Grant's desert golden mole, for example, digs long, winding tunnels under the dunes. It noses aside loose sand with its leathery snout. This snout is the only noticeable feature on its face. As the golden mole glides beneath the sand, it snatches legless lizards and insects above it and pulls them into its burrow to eat.

Another desert dweller, the blind snake, can burrow through loose sand even though it has no limbs for digging. It uses a spike at the end of its body to help push itself along. During the day, this snake stays beneath the surface. At night, it skims across the sand.

In East Africa, a pink, almost hairless rat tunnels like a mole. It looks like a sausage with two buck teeth. Called the naked mole rat, it has a complex social system similar to that of some insects. A female, the queen, rules each underground colony of 80 or more members. Their home is a system of many tunnels with a large central nesting area. To burrow through the earth, members of the

ANTHONY BANNISTER (BELOW AND OPPOSITE TOP)

△ The smooth head of a Grant's desert golden mole pushes up from the sand. Fur protects this burrowing animal's eyes and ears. The golden mole hunts by sensing movement in the sand.

◁ S-shaped patterns mark the path of a blind snake. It often escapes the desert heat by traveling underground.

◁ Flying soil signals that naked mole rats are tunneling below. Various members of the colony cooperate in digging, finding food, and raising young.

▷ With only a few hairs and mole-like habits, this rat is well named. It is called the naked mole rat. Its two large front teeth are good tools for gnawing on roots and bulbs.

worker class form a line. Then they dig together as a team. Each one kicks a load of soil to the one behind it. The last in line kicks it outside the tunnel and then scrambles over the others to get to the head of the line. There, the whole process begins again.

Underground animals include some spiders as well. They are found around the world, especially in warm climates, including southern and western parts of the United States.

The trap-door spider, for example, uses the hard, rake-like bristles on its jaws for scraping out a tunnel. Then the spider coats the walls with a mixture of soil and saliva. Next comes a lining of silk spun from the spider's body. Later the spider makes a door of silk, sometimes strengthening it with earth. A silk hinge attaches the door to the burrow entrance. Finally the spider camouflages the outside of the door with bits of soil and plants.

Their burrows protect trap-door spiders from sun, rain, cold, and the wasps that prey on them. Safe inside, the spiders are able to sense the slightest movement outside. Movement may mean that an insect is nearby. To spiders, insects *(Continued on page 88)*

◁ *A female trap-door spider lines her tunnel walls with silk. A flimsy trapdoor—made of silk and camouflaged with leaves, moss, and grass—covers the entrance. This rare kind of trap-door spider has a large, leathery abdomen. She can use her tough abdomen as a shield to protect herself from enemies.*

▷ *A trap-door spider— only 1 inch (2$\frac{1}{2}$ cm) long—peers from her burrow. This kind of trap-door spider makes a strong door of silk webbing and earth. Here, she has opened the door after sensing a movement outside.*

84

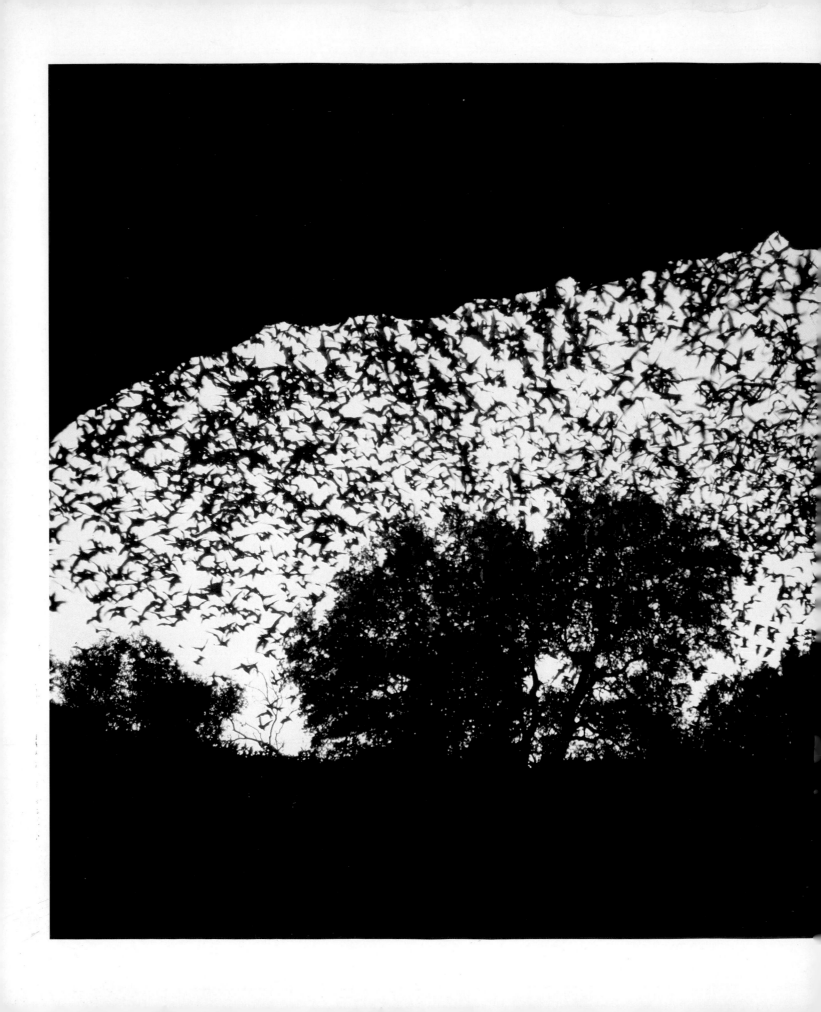

◁ Outlined against the sky, thousands of Mexican free-tailed bats fly from a cave at dusk. They're off on their nightly search for insects. Bats are an important part of the life in some caves. Their rich droppings are the main food source for many small creatures that live in the caves.

▽ Cave explorer Karen Tarnow crawls under a curtain of stone. This formation resulted when dripping water left behind minerals. The minerals slowly built up to form the curtain. "A cave is a whole different world," says Karen. "It's fascinating how animals survive there."

KERRY T. GIVENS

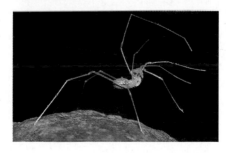

◁ A harvestman, or daddy longlegs, feels its way with sensitive legs. This pale, blind variety of harvestman is a cave dweller. Over a long period of time, the harvestman adapted to the total darkness of caves. It lost its sight and its color.

87

(*Continued from page 84*) mean lunch. For a quick meal, trap-door spiders push open their trapdoors and grab passing insects.

Caves are another part of the secret world of animals. A number of animals, including some kinds of spiders, have adapted to life there. It's dark and very quiet, except for the dripping of water. If you joined a caving expedition, you might spot some of the creatures that make their homes in caves.

Near the cave entrance, you might see bats, spiders, and insects. They take shelter inside, but at times they leave to find food. If you traveled deeper, you'd come to an area where sunlight never reaches. With luck, you might spot a troglobite (TRAHG-luh-bite). That's the name for an animal that spends its entire life in a cave. It might be a strange-looking salamander or a pale, blind crayfish.

In this chapter, you have peeked into burrows, tunnels, and caves, and you've seen how underground animals get along in their environments. In a dark tunnel, for example, a good nose or sensitive body hairs are more important than keen eyesight. Adaptations such as these are the keys to survival underground.

△ *Pale copy of its above-ground relatives, the cave crayfish lives in pools and streams inside caves. Sunlight never reaches it. In the dark, color and vision serve no purpose so—over long periods of time—these creatures became colorless and blind.*

▷ *Feathery gills decorate the head of a Tennessee cave salamander. The salamander's ancestors might have first entered caves for shelter, or they might have been washed in during a flood. Now, this kind of salamander lives only in caves.*

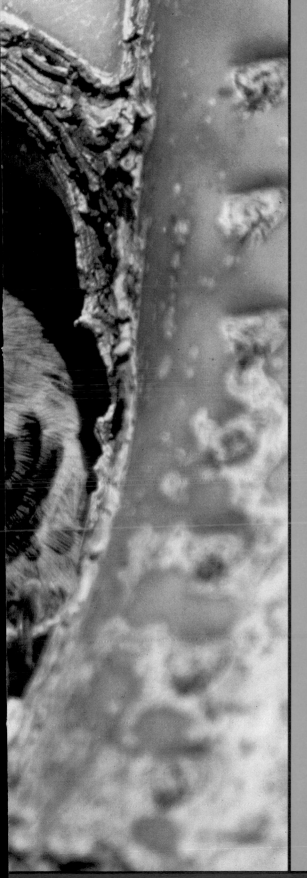

INSIDE ANIMAL

HOTELS

By Susan McGrath

Have you ever stayed in a hotel—perhaps while on vacation? Animals don't take vacations, of course, but sometimes they stay in "hotels" as a matter of survival. In this chapter, you'll see different kinds of animals checking in at the same hotel.

N.G.S. PHOTOGRAPHER GEORGE F. MOBLEY

Towering above the Sonoran Desert, for example, in parts of Arizona, California, and Mexico are giant, branching cactuses called saguaros (suh-WAHR-ohz). Some of these high-rise hotels are 200 years old and stand taller than most houses. If you took a close look at one, you might spot as many as 40 small holes high up in its trunk and branches. Over the years, such holes—the rooms of the saguaro hotel—are chiseled out by two kinds of woodpeckers, the Gila (HEE-la) woodpecker and the northern flicker.

When a woodpecker makes a nest hole in a saguaro, sap oozes from the walls of the cavity. The sticky sap hardens into a woody lining. The entrance hole—as small as a golf ball or as large as a baseball—leads to a gourd-shaped cavity. There, the woodpecker

Young northern flickers peer out of their nest high in a saguaro cactus. Saguaros (above) can grow as tall as five-story buildings in about 150 years. Vacant woodpecker holes provide shelter for other birds, for bats, and for insects. The saguaro is a high-rise hotel for animals of the Sonoran Desert.

JEN AND DES BARTLETT/BRUCE COLEMAN LTD. (LEFT)

91

lays its eggs and raises its young. Woodpeckers chisel new holes every year, so the number of rooms constantly increases.

Birds that can't dig out their own nests move into those abandoned by the woodpeckers. As many as 16 other species of birds live in the saguaro hotel at various times—elf owls, purple martins, and wrens, to name a few. Most of them lay their eggs directly on the cavity floor without using nesting material.

Birds are not the only guests at this hotel. Bats sometimes check in for a nap during the heat of the day. Mice move into rooms at lower levels of the saguaro. The eggs of a certain kind of mosquito develop in holes that become filled with rainwater.

The rooms of the saguaro hotel have natural air-conditioning. The thick walls of the cactus keep out the desert heat during the day and the cold at night. Water stored in the tissue of the cactus keeps the air inside the cavities more moist than the outside desert air. As a result, animals living in a saguaro don't need much water. You can see why this hotel is popular with many desert animals. It helps them survive the harsh conditions. _ (Continued on page 96)

▽ *A saguaro sculptor, the Gila woodpecker pauses at its nest hole. When a woodpecker chisels into a saguaro, sap oozes out and hardens to form a tough nest lining. In exchange for a room, the woodpecker helps the cactus by eating insects that may be harmful to it.*

△ *Doves feast on ripe red saguaro fruit. They help the cactus by spreading its seeds in their droppings. A saguaro produces as many as 12 million seeds in its lifetime, but scientists estimate that only one seed will produce a full-size cactus—a process that takes 150 years.*

▷ *An elf owlet about as big as your fist stares from its room in a saguaro hotel. Elf owls move into vacant woodpecker nests as high as 40 feet (12 m) above the ground. From there, the owls have a good view of prey, such as centipedes. They can be longer than the elf owl is tall!*

C. ALLAN MORGAN (BOTH)

HOTEL ON THE RANGE

Scattered beneath the prairie's surface are burrow systems constructed by prairie dogs. Cooler in summer and warmer in winter than the prairie above them, these hotels on the range are used by many kinds of animals. Some live there year-round. Others just visit when searching for food or shelter.

94

This painting shows a cross section of a small portion of a prairie dog town in early summer. A burrowing owl covers its unhatched eggs with its wings while a newly hatched owlet stands nearby. The father peers out of their tunnel opening. A prairie rattlesnake hunts for a mouse while avoiding the heat at the surface. In winter, dozens of these rattlers may hibernate in a single chamber.

The almost extinct black-footed ferret (lower left) lives only in prairie dog hotels. Ferrets sleep at the edge of the community. They usually hunt at night, but a female ferret with young to feed may hunt around the clock. She sometimes enters more than a hundred holes a day looking for a prairie dog to eat. In the maze of tunnels, speedy prairie dogs may be able to escape a hungry ferret.

A cottontail rabbit, chased by a coyote, finds temporary shelter in a nearby hole. The North American badger (upper right)—unlike the ferret— does not enter the hotel's passageways. Rather, it digs into burrows in its search for prairie dogs.

In a nesting chamber, prairie dog pups wait for their mother while other members of the community look and listen for danger.

95

(Continued from page 92) Without the saguaro cactuses, many animals could not live in the Sonoran Desert.

Another kind of animal hotel exists on North American grasslands. In summer, these nearly treeless prairies can heat up like furnaces. In winter, icy winds and snow sweep across them. Beneath areas of the prairie lie systems of chambers and tunnels constructed by prairie dogs. Without these hotels, many kinds of animals would have no protection from weather or from predators.

If you sat quietly at the edge of a black-tailed prairie dog town in the summertime, you'd probably see young prairie dogs playing in the low grass. You might also see a long-legged burrowing owl scrambling into an abandoned prairie dog burrow with insects for its young. Perhaps you would see prairie rattlesnakes sunning themselves or slithering in and out of the town looking for mice.

If you were very lucky, you'd catch a glimpse of a sleek black-footed ferret slipping into burrow after burrow in search of prairie dogs. Although prairie dogs might prefer *not* to share their hotel with black-footed ferrets, these members of the weasel family

FRANZ J. CAMENZIND

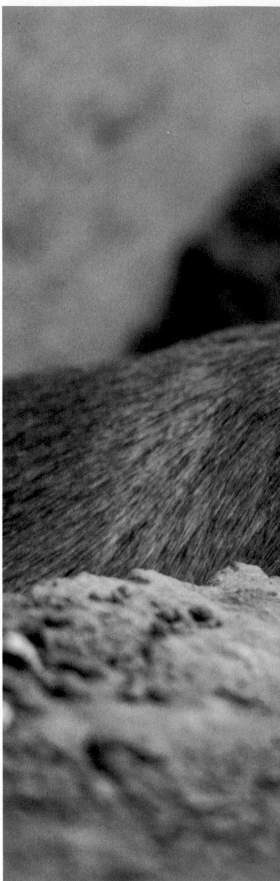

△ *The black-footed ferret needs the prairie dog as food and its town as shelter. When people and disease started killing prairie dogs, the ferrets began to die out. Now, very few survive.*

▷ *A prairie dog suns itself at an entrance to its town. Such underground hotels play an important role in life on the prairie. Without them, many animals would not have shelter.*

96

cannot survive without prairie dogs—their primary source of food. To many ranchers, prairie dogs are pests. Their towns—with their many holes and mounds—make acres of land unusable for grazing. By poisoning the prairie dogs, ranchers indirectly have almost wiped out the black-footed ferrets. A disease carried by fleas also sometimes kills prairie dogs. Robbed of their favorite food, the ferrets are now almost extinct.

A much simpler version of an underground hotel exists in the hot, dry sandhills of north-central Florida and nearby states. There, the gopher tortoise is the master digger. It uses its flat front legs and strong nails to dig its burrow. Then it uses its shell like a bulldozer to push the sand outside. Gradually, the tortoise excavates a tunnel about 30 feet (9 m) long and 5 to 9 feet (1½ to 3 m) below the earth's surface. During the heat of the day, the tortoise stays in a room at the end of the tunnel. During cooler hours, it comes out to feed.

In the territory of the gopher tortoise, the sand can become scorching hot. Often, grass fires blaze up. It can be a tough place to live. Many kinds of animals in the Florida sandhills survive only by

▽ *A scientist holding an adult gopher tortoise wears a T-shirt that illustrates a gopher tortoise's hotel. It shows the plants and the sandy soil typical of the environment. In the drawing, the tortoise has laid her eggs beside the burrow entrance. In real life, she would have covered them with sand. Inside the hotel are a snake, a gopher frog, and a tortoise—the hotel owner.*

FIONA SUNQUIST (ALL)

△ *With its sharp-edged mouth, a gopher tortoise snaps off plants. A vegetarian, this tortoise is no threat to its guests. Although it has powerful, shovel-like front feet, it uses them for digging, not for attacking prey. The shell of the tortoise helps protect it from predators.*

▷ *A gopher tortoise approaches the opening to its burrow. The entrance tunnel is usually as wide as the tortoise is long—about 1 foot (⅓ m)—and about 30 feet (9 m) long. At the end is a chamber. The burrow protects not only the tortoise but other animals as well.*

98

taking shelter in the gopher tortoise hotel. Snakes, gopher frogs, Florida mice, and insects are only a few of the many kinds of animals that live there year-round. Some occupy the main chamber with the tortoise. Others live in small side chambers. A number of larger animals—armadillos, raccoons, foxes, and opossums—occasionally visit the gopher tortoise hotel to find food or to escape grass fires. Some enlarge vacant burrows to use as nurseries.

When different species live together, the arrangement is called symbiosis (sim-by-OH-sis). In this chapter, you have seen several examples of such relationships. Symbiosis may be either beneficial or harmful to the animals involved. Sometimes it is neither. Animals that build hotels simply make the homes they themselves need to survive, but their efforts often benefit others.

Now that you've seen how creatures use burrows, caves, and tree cavities, see how many animal hideaways you can spot. Be a nature detective and you'll discover some of the wonders hidden in the secret world of animals. Look and listen for clues—but do not disturb the shelters you find. The animals depend on them for survival.

FIONA SUNQUIST (BOTH)

△ *A guest at an animal hotel, an opossum crawls out of a gopher tortoise burrow. Such burrows are cool places for opossums to rest during the heat of the day. They—and many other animals—also use the burrows to escape the frequent grass fires that sweep over the Florida sandhills.*

▷ *A gopher frog and a Florida mouse come face-to-face in a gopher tortoise burrow. These two species live only in the tortoise's sandhills hotel. The Florida mouse makes its home in a tiny side tunnel (center). The mouse can plug the tunnel to keep out snakes and other predators.*

100

INDEX

Bold type refers to illustrations; regular type refers to text.

ADDITIONAL READING

Readers may want to check the *National Geographic Index* and the *World Index* in a school or a public library for related articles. These volumes in the National Geographic Society's Books for World Explorers series also contain related material: *How Animals Behave: A New Look at Wildlife; Secrets of Animal Survival;* and *Wildlife Alert! The Struggle to Survive.* Readers may also want to refer to the Society's *The Desert Realm; The Marvels of Animal Behavior;* the *National Geographic Book of Mammals, Vols. 1 and 2;* and *Wild Animals of North America,* as well as to the following books for young readers ("A" indicates a book for readers at the adult level):

Arnosky, Jim, *Secrets of a Wildlife Watcher,* Lothrop, Lee & Shepard Books, 1983. Bailey, Bernadine, *Wonders of the World of Bears,* Dodd, Mead & Company, 1975. Bancroft, Henrietta, and Richard G. Van Gelder, *Animals in Winter,* Thomas Y. Crowell Co., 1963. Bare, Colleen Stanley, *The Durable Desert Tortoise,* Dodd, Mead & Company, 1979. Barlowe, Dot and Sy, *Who Lives Here?* Random House, 1978.

Blassingame, Wyatt, *The Strange Armadillo,* Dodd, Mead & Company, 1983; *Wonders of Raccoons,* Dodd, Mead & Company, 1977. *The Cats,* Time-Life Films, 1976. Chase, G. Earl, *Wonders of Prairie Dogs,* Dodd, Mead & Company, 1976. Clarke, Anne, *Rabbit,* William Heinemann Ltd., in association with the British Museum, 1981. Conklin, Gladys, *Insects Build Their Homes,* Holiday House, 1972. Cosgrove, Margaret, *Animals Alone and Together: Their Solitary and Social Lives,* Dodd, Mead & Company, 1978.

Costello, David F., *The World of the Prairie Dog,* J. B. Lippincott Company, 1970. Cowan, David, *The Wild Rabbit,* Blandford Press, in association with the Mammal Society, 1980. Deegan, Paul, *Animals of East Africa,* Creative Education, Inc., 1971. Earnest, Don, *Rabbits & Other Small Mammals,* Time-Life Films, 1978. Eastman, Rosemary, *The Kingfisher,* Collins Clear-Type Press, 1969. Eugene, J. Walter, Jr., *Why Animals Behave the Way They Do,* Charles Scribner's Sons, 1981.

Evans, Howard, and Mary J. Eberhard, *The Wasps,* University of Michigan Press, 1970 (A). Farb, Peter, *The Insects,* Time-Life Books Inc., 1980 (A). Friedman, Judi, *Puffins, Come Back!* Dodd, Mead & Company, 1981. Gertsch, Willis J., *American Spiders,* Van Nostrand Reinhold Company, 1979 (A). Gustafson, Anita, *Burrowing Birds,* Lothrop, Lee & Shepard Books, 1981. Haley, Patrick, *The Woodpecker & the Oak Tree,* East Eagle Press, 1982. Hancocks, David, *Master Builders of the Animal World,* Hugh Evelyn Ltd., 1973 (A).

Hartman, Jane E., *How Animals Care for Their Young,* Holiday House, 1980; *Living Together in Nature: How Symbiosis Works,* Holiday House, 1977. Hutchins, Ross E., *A Look at ANTS,* Dodd, Mead & Company, 1978. Jackson, Donald, *Underground Worlds,* Time-Life Books Inc., 1982 (A). Jacobson, Morris K., and David R. Franz, *Wonders of Snails & Slugs,* Dodd, Mead & Company, 1980.

Johnson, Sylvia A., *Crabs,* Lerner Publications Co., 1982. Kohl, Judith and Herbert, *Pack, Band, & Colony: The World of Social Animals,* Farrar, Straus & Giroux, Inc., 1983; *The View from the Oak,* Sierra Club, 1977. Larson, Peggy, *Deserts of America,* Prentice-Hall, Inc., 1970. Larson, Peggy P. and

Mervin W., *All About Ants,* Thomas Y. Crowell Co., 1976. Lauber, Patricia, *Life on a Giant Cactus,* Garrard Publishing Co., 1974. Lavine, Sigmund A., *Wonders of Badgers,* Dodd, Mead & Company, 1985; *Wonders of Coyotes,* Dodd, Mead & Company, 1984.

Laycock, George, *Bats in the Night,* Four Winds Press, 1981. Leon, Dorothy, *The Secret World of Underground Creatures,* Julian Messner, 1982. Leopold, A. Starker, *The Desert,* Time-Life Books Inc., 1980 (A). Lockley, R. M., *The Private Life of the Rabbit,* Macmillan Publishing Co., Inc., 1974 (A). McDearmon, Kay, *Cougar,* Dodd, Mead & Company, 1977; *Foxes,* Dodd, Mead & Company, 1981. McFarland, David, editor, *The Oxford Companion to Animal Behaviour,* Oxford University Press, 1981 (A).

Mason, George F., *Animal Homes,* William Morrow & Co., Inc., 1956. Milne, Lorus and Margery, *Gadabouts and Stick-at-Homes,* Charles Scribner's Sons, 1980. Mohr, Charles E., and Thomas L. Poulson, *The Life of the Cave,* McGraw-Hill, 1966 (A). Morris, Dean, *Animals That Burrow,* Raintree Publications, Inc., 1984. Neal, Ernest G., *Badgers,* Blandford Press, 1977 (A). Neary, John, *Insects & Spiders,* Time-Life Films, 1977. Nussbaum, Hilda, *Animals Build Amazing Homes,* Random House, Inc., 1975. Oulahan, Richard, *Reptiles & Amphibians,* Time-Life Films, 1976. Overback, Cynthia, *Ants,* Lerner Publications Co., 1982.

Peterson, Roger Tory, *The Birds,* Time-Life Books Inc., 1980 (A). Rebel, Thomas P., *Sea Turtles,* University of Miami Press, 1974 (A). Riedman, Sarah R., *Odd Habitats of Land Animals,* David McKay Company, Inc., 1980. Riedman, Sarah R., and Ross Witham, *Turtles: Extinction or Survival?* Abelard-Schuman, 1974. Roberts, Allan, *Underground Life,* Childrens Press, 1983. Rockwell, Jane, *Wolves,* Franklin Watts, Inc., 1977. Rue, Leonard Lee, III, *The World of the Raccoon,* J. B. Lippincott Company, 1964. Scott, Jack Denton, and Ozzie Sweet, *Little Dogs of the Prairie,* G. P. Putnam's Sons, 1977. Selsam, Millicent E., *Where Do They Go? Insects in Winter,* Four Winds Press, 1982. Short, Lester L., *Woodpeckers of the World,* Delaware Museum of Natural History, 1982 (A).

Simon, Hilda, *Snails of Land and Sea,* The Vanguard Press, 1976. Simon, Seymour, *Discovering What Garter Snakes Do,* McGraw-Hill, 1975; *Life in the Dark,* Franklin Watts, 1974. Spoczynska, Joy D., *The World of the Wasp,* Crane, Russak & Co., Inc., 1975. Stonehouse, Bernard, *Young Animals: The Search for Independent Life,* Viking Press, Inc., 1974. Taketazu, Minoru, *Fox Family, Four Seasons of Animal Life,* John Weatherhill, Inc., 1979. Tanner, Ogden, *Bears & Other Carnivores,* Time-Life Films, 1976. Teale, Edwin Way, *The Junior Book of Insects,* E. P. Dutton & Co., Inc., 1972. Tinbergen, Niko, *Animal Behavior,* Time-Life Books Inc., 1980 (A).

Von Frisch, Karl, *Animal Architecture,* Harcourt Brace Jovanovich, 1974 (A). Walker, Lewis Wayne, *The Book of Owls,* Alfred A. Knopf, 1974. Whitfield, Philip, *The Animal Family,* W. W. Norton & Co., Inc., 1980. Wildlife Education Ltd., *Night Animals,* Wildlife Education, Ltd., 1984. Williams, Austin B., *Shrimps, Lobsters, & Crabs of the Atlantic Coast of the Eastern United States, Maine to Florida,* Smithsonian Institution Press, 1984 (A).

CONSULTANTS

William A. Xanten, Jr., National Zoological Park, *Chief Consultant*; Fiona Sunquist, *Contributing Consultant*

Glenn O. Blough, LL.D. Emeritus Professor of Education, University of Maryland, *Educational Consultant*

Joan Myers, Alexandria City (Virginia) Public Schools, *Reading Consultant*

Nicholas J. Long, Ph.D., *Consulting Psychologist*

The Special Publications and School Services Division is grateful to the individuals and organizations listed here for their generous cooperation and assistance during the preparation of THE SECRET WORLD OF ANIMALS:

C. Michael Bailey, National Aquarium, Washington, D. C.; Andrew J. Baker; Tim W. Clark, Biota; Jonathan Coddington, Smithsonian Institution; Stephen T. Emlen, Cornell University; Howard E. Evans, Colorado State University; Gregory Florant, Swarthmore College; Richard Franz, Florida State Museum; Gary R. Graves, Smithsonian Institution; Thomas R. Howell, University of California, Los Angeles; W. Thomas Jones; Stephen W. Kress, National Audubon Society; Karl V. Krombein, Smithsonian Institution; Scott Larcher, Smithsonian Institution; Roy McDiarmid, U. S. Fish and Wildlife Service; Arnold S. Menke, U. S. Department of Agriculture; Robert Mitchell; Ernest G. Neal; Robert O. Petty, Wabash College; Charles Pickett, National Zoological Park; C. Jenny Ryon, Dalhousie University; D. Peter Siminski, Arizona-Sonora Desert Museum; David R. Smith, U. S. Department of Agriculture; Louis N. Sorkin, American Museum of Natural History; Karen Tarnow; Austin B. Williams, National Marine Fisheries Service; F. E. Wood, University of Maryland.

Composition for THE SECRET WORLD OF ANIMALS by National Geographic's Photographic Services, Carl M. Shrader, Director; Lawrence F. Ludwig, Assistant Director. Printed and bound by Holladay-Tyler Printing Corp., Rockville, Md. Color separations by the Lanman-Progressive Co., Washington, D. C.; Lincoln Graphics, Inc., Cherry Hill, N.J.

Library of Congress CIP Data
   The Secret world of animals.
   (Books for world explorers)
   Bibliography: p.
   Includes index.
   Summary: Text and pictures take the reader inside animal homes—used for resting, sheltering from weather, escaping enemies, and raising young.
      1. Animals—Habitations—Juvenile literature.
   [1. Animals—Habitations] I. Series.
   QL756.S38   1986   591.56′4   86-5141
   ISBN 0-87044-575-8 (regular edition)
   ISBN 0-87044-580-4 (library edition)

The Secret World of Animals

PUBLISHED BY
THE NATIONAL GEOGRAPHIC SOCIETY
WASHINGTON, D. C.

Gilbert M. Grosvenor, *President*
Melvin M. Payne, *Chairman of the Board*
Owen R. Anderson, *Executive Vice President*
Robert L. Breeden, *Senior Vice President
Publications and Educational Media*

PREPARED BY THE SPECIAL PUBLICATIONS
AND SCHOOL SERVICES DIVISION
Donald J. Crump, *Director*
Philip B. Silcott, *Associate Director*
Bonnie S. Lawrence, *Assistant Director*

BOOKS FOR WORLD EXPLORERS
Pat Robbins, *Editor*
Ralph Gray, *Editor Emeritus*
Margaret McKelway, *Associate Editor*
Ursula Perrin Vosseler, *Art Director*

STAFF FOR THE SECRET WORLD OF ANIMALS
Martha C. Christian, *Managing Editor*
Veronica J. Morrison, *Picture Editor*
Mary E. Molloy, *Art Director*
Suzanne Nave Patrick, *Senior Editorial Researcher*
Gail Nathena Hawkins, *Researcher*
Patricia N. Holland, *Special Projects Editor*
Joan Hurst, *Editorial Assistant*
Artemis S. Lampathakis, *Senior Illustrations Assistant*
Bernadette L. Grigonis, *Illustrations Assistant*

ENGRAVING, PRINTING, AND PRODUCT MANUFACTURE: Robert W. Messer, *Manager*; David V. Showers, *Production Manager*; Gregory Storer, *Production Project Manager*; Mark R. Dunlevy, George J. Zeller, Jr., *Assistant Production Managers*; Timothy H. Ewing, *Production Assistant*

STAFF ASSISTANTS: Mary Brennan, Vicki L. Broom, Carol R. Curtis, Lori Elizabeth Davie, Mary Elizabeth Davis, Ann Di Fiore, Rosamund Garner, Virginia W. Hannasch, Nancy J. Harvey, Katherine R. Leitch, Ann E. Newman, Cleo E. Petroff, Stuart E. Pfitzinger, Virginia A. Williams

MARKET RESEARCH: Mark W. Brown, Joseph S. Fowler, Carrla L. Holmes, Meg M. Keiffer, Barbara Steinwurtzel, Marsha Sussman, Judy Turnbull

INDEX: Stephany J. Freedman